ISBN: 9781313278294

Published by:
HardPress Publishing
8345 NW 66TH ST #2561
MIAMI FL 33166-2626

Email: info@hardpress.net
Web: http://www.hardpress.net

A LEAGUE OF JUSTICE

OR

IS IT RIGHT TO ROB ROBBERS?

BY

MORRISON I. SWIFT.

PRICE FIFTY CENTS.

BOSTON
THE COMMONWEALTH SOCIETY
9 NASSAU STREET
1893

CONTENTS.

A LEAGUE OF JUSTICE.

CHAPTER I.

THE LEAGUE GARDENING THE ROOTS OF THE SOCIAL SYSTEM.

Four men met together in the garret where one of them lived. They were the trusted clerks of great commercial houses. Through the hands of each passed daily sums equal to fortunes. They were men of devoted honesty; not one but would have died rather than take for himself a penny of his employers' funds. The salary of two of these men was nine hundred dollars a year. The others received one thousand each. They were also allowed a vacation of two weeks in the summer. With families or friends to support, their salaries did not take them far from the town during this resting time. They were not old men, but a look of age was upon each of their faces, and all were prematurely gray.

They spoke with grave faces. Evidently they had come too far in life to act from ill-balanced enthusiasm. They took no oath of fidelity to one another, nor to the cause they were undertaking. An oath would not have deepened their loyalty.

One of them said: "If we are skillful and do not take amounts too large, we may hope to escape detection five or even ten years. Soon or late each will be discovered, imprisoned and his family disgraced. Is the cause worthy of this sacrifice?"

"It is," they responded in firm tones.

They remained in conference two hours arranging the plans of their work.

A month later ten men assembled in the same garret. The society had grown through the admission of six comrades. The four founders reported their progress.

"I have taken one thousand dollars," "I eight hundred," "I thirteen hundred," "I two thousand dollars," they said in turns.

The first speaker continued: "My most difficult part has been to distribute what I took. I helped several destitute families, but with inadequate sums, for fear of the suspicious question, where I came by the money. But through a friend who does not ask questions, I saved a hard working market gardener from losing his little plot of ground through mortgage. I have five hundred dollars left."

The others made similar reports.

"This difficulty is already disposed of," the president said. "One has joined us who is not a clerk, and who can be our distributing agent, judiciously applying what sums are needed without drawing suspicion to himself or us. He may pass as the representative of philanthropic but modest persons who do not wish their names known, dispersing his assistance over the city to avoid suggestive comparisons."

New names were considered, and several were rejected, lacking the high reliability of character necessary to sustain an arduous mission. Against the emergency of general exposure from a member proving untrustworthy, it was resolved to develop the society in separate and wholly independent groups of ten, the four original organizers, only, being authorized to initiate groups, and they alone knowing the entire membership. For the rest, each one's knowledge was to be limited to his own group. Should a member be false, his testimony could at worst convict his nine associates only, and the progress of the society would not be impaired. Each section was to have its own distributor.

"If a group and its processes are discovered," said one, "other groups are endangered, for detectives will scent out recipients of aid and snare those who furnish it."

"And if an agent was discovered, what then? We may be sure he would never betray his comrades. But we can trust them to baffle detection: they can disguise themselves, or invent a visit and leave money unnoticed; a child met outside the door will never refuse to carry a package to its parents; and there is the mail, too, which would hardly suspect a common brown parcel of containing crisp bills; and if these strategies wear threadbare, think of the hundreds of stores anxious to sell a yard of cloth and deliver it, and quite obliging enough to wrap in another thing or two if you please. That part is easy enough. A shrewd distributor is quite out of reach of discovery."

So answered another to this seeming obstacle.

To comprehend the beneficent successes of these self-abegnating men, we must follow their agent in his novel excursions. In many disguises he learned the true conditian of scores of poor families. He adopted a special character for each district. Being a physician, he appeared in one quarter of the city in this guise; in another he was an authorized sanitary inspector; to a third he went as a student investigating; to another as an advising clergyman; and one locality knew him as a statistician for the labor union to which he belonged. The sums that he disposed of in a section were not large enough to arouse comment. He found many families falling behind in rent, through the sickness of their breadwinners, with the gray prospect near of being forced to surrender bad quarters for worse ones, and he banished that evil phantom. There were widows in almost every tenement, who left their colorless children daily to wear out their fragile strength in factories for the comfort of their landlords, and to buy off death from the immediate execution of their infants by the sufferings of miserable maturity. They were conveyed to country towns, housed there and clothed, and a year's rent paid for them. The number of half-clad children for whom he provided warm flannels would not be credited by the fabulously righteous slummers and charity supervisors; and where there were persons whose miniature wages declined to pay for a nourishing dinner once a week, he contrived to astonish them with immaculate sections of beef on days that were not holidays.

Let not the generous reader imagine that this rising and energetic providence fed all the needy people; a galaxy of unretired providences, giving their attention to business, was requisite for that, and it came in good time.

For it was not many years before there were branches of this beneficent institution in every prominent city of the North, West, East and South, Chicago leading, as in all good things, with a full hundred; and the groups began to specialize their undertakings, some of them being fond of presenting the tenement artisans with snug farms in the west and seeing their proteges safely settled there, protected from the pirating land-speculators of that fringe of paradise, and their intriguing colleagues in the banks.

But nothing told so powerfully and swiftly for the amelioration of the laboring millions as the gold which certain far-sighted groups knew how to pour into the treasuries of strikers; and from that date an astonishing success began to crown the participators in labor wars. This invention in the mechanics of social progress rose to its legitimate importance through the signal victory it enabled workingmen to win over one Carnegie, now forgotten, but at that period of his life a famous exploiter of labor and legislation. This ambitions person, who sought distinction as a patron simultaneously of statesmen, starvelings and an envious rout of middle-minded people, cut from the Anglo-Saxon pattern, whose genius lay in unsuccessfully wishing to exploit contemporary mankind of millions and loyally supporting those who successfully exploited them. This individual, blessed with an environment of propitious clay and the courage of his instinct that thousands were born to minister to his gayety and aggrandizement, determined, as Napoleon once determined to shatter Russia, to crush the labor organizations out of his pathway to democratic fraternity and sovereignty; for he knew that if these thorny impediments in the mills which he was fond of considering his own were brushed aside, he could manage the vulgar rabble of wage-earners to his heart's desire, and gaining ever more wealth from their unwilling contributions, and buying ever more honor and grandeur from the world's grocery where these nourishing articles are sold, and disbursing his eminent talents and profits so far as business allowed, he would at length grow to the size of the gods and live in men's memories with Jesus and Plato and Gould. To enjoy the virtuous consciousness of well-earned wealth and philosophic freedom from the physical evils besetting the course of one who heroically destroys the aspirations of hamlets of human beings, whose poetry is the blast furnace and whose philosophic excursions are the peripatetic synthesis of broiling iron, he betook himself to a fair castle in distant Scotland—a house not made with his own hands, but bought with the labor of his hands at Homestead, whom now, teeming with thankful devices, he was pondering keen-edged thoughts to degrade.

It was just at this moment that certain ethical groups, pursuing rectitude, became awake to their opportunity and began to contribute to the strikers' support. All non-union men who, being out of work, came to fill the places of the old hands, were enrolled upon the pay list of the others and refused to go to work. The aid which was given sufficed to keep the strikers from want, and perceiving that some powerful popular sentiment was back of them, they continued firm in their formerly unequal struggle with sceptred capital. It was the turning point of that struggle, for the most swollen potentates of finance could not survive the losses which Carnegie suffered for a protracted period. When at length he yielded, to avoid ruin, the men were not content to resume their posts with trifling concessions in wages and acknowledgement of the right to combine. Their compulsory idleness has educated them, and understanding for the first time their power, they negotiated a partnership with their previous master. The influence of this Waterloo to a shining knight of capital upon the country, was like the dazzling rise of a competing sun in the horizon.

Strikers in other places were not neglected, and the proportion of successful strikes rapidly swelled. It broke upon the esoteric inkiness of the employers' brain that strikes were stunning their trade and almost uniformly succeeding, and they grew very chary of putting the vitals of the cumbersome beast, capital, under the club of the executioner; wherefore, strikes decreased with acceleration, the employers preferring reasonable concessions to their own economic extinction. These concessions in turn produced a notable improvement in the condition and character of the employes. Seeing the unmistakable success of the labor organizations, workmen who had refused to join in earlier days, shrinking from the displeasure of their all-potent employing dictators, rallied to the unions, augmenting still further their vitality and beneficence. The capitalists sadly saw that when the unions composed themselves for a strike, they were predestined to win, and they shaped their shriveling course accordingly. On their part, rejoicing in their April potency, and recognizing the immense physical and moral dividends of each material increment to their class, the unions began to prepare themselves for more considerable alleviations touching social and material equality.

CHAPTER II.

BRAINS AND CAPITALISTS FALL OUT.

In the meantime, production itself was feeling a change. Demand for the necessaries of life had grown with the grown incomes of the poor, and employment for a fresh army corps of working people sprang up in these industries. Demand for luxuries had declined, but not in proportion to the increased demands for comforts and necessaries, and the volume of business as a whole was greater by far than ever before. Capitalists had discovered a shrinkage in their incomes, and not being able to account for it in any other way, had supposed it was because the industrial share of labor had increased. The wise had curtailed their superfluity expenses and were healthier and happier; the foolish, not being able to curtail, failed, and their business passed to the hands of men with less regal sentiments of their own deserts and new ideas about the proportion labor merits. The wisest of all, finding society so much more wholesome since the workers began to advance, came out boldly as labor champions and made their factories co-operative.

Nevertheless, despite the large deductions which the members of the League of Justice were making from the gross "earnings" of the capitalists, their net incomes fell off in no very marked manner, for the productive capacity and quality of the working population rose so steadily, in consequence of their better material state, that they rendered to the employers in return for wages, a larger product than ever before. This tended to reconcile the masters to the laborers' daily enlarging demands. And, moreover, if some capital had been withdrawn from the manufacture of luxuries, still more having been invested in the manufacture of necessaries and comforts, capital enjoyed satisfying returns from this.

The entire bulk of capital was swelled in another way undreamed of by the worthy wealthies of previous times. It had been a principle entirely undisputed by prelates, professors and practical men, that the cause of the poverty of the poor was their heedless and immense expenditures upon frivolities and vices, men receiving a dollar a day to nurture a family with being supposed to spend four or five dollars of that sum daily for beer and brawling, and the capitalists suffered so terribly from this enormous waste that they feared all the factories and savings of the country would be drunk up and production would cease because the capital was gone, unless they cut down the wages of the workers still more and applied the saved surplus to their own scant domestic outlays and recuperative investments in private wines and diamonds for the preservation of capital. Now it was ascertained, to the confusion of all the good and thrifty, that so soon as the working people found themselves in fair health and comfort with their better food and homes, they began to save, and had the good lords of earth, the prelates of heaven, and the professors of both, not been retarded in speaking by the emerald scum of jealousy rising in their throats, they would have admitted that a good lump of the savings, so-called, which the rich had squandered in fruitless famous extravagances, became now an accumulation among the workers, actually saved for the enhancement of production. And ownership being distributed among many, multiplied the benefits which it bestowed.

Their new intelligence enabled them to shake the citadel of the middle-man and the sweating boss-contractor, for they found that they themselves could take group contracts as in Australia, instead of letting some ravenous overseer exploit them as hired workers. And it soon came about that they could obtain any contract for which they applied, since their superior ability and the excellence and reliability of their work rendered all they did more profitable to employers than the slipshod profligate constructions of contractors. They could underbid if they wished, saving from the contractor's plutonic profits and stealings.

They began to invest their savings in manufactories of their own, which they conducted without sharing the profits with any idle club of capitalists, stock-holders, or managers, with sky-reaching salaries. Such enterprises grew apace, for they could undersell the manufactories which had the terrible corporation of capitalists and 'managers' on their backs. Formerly the capitalists had all things their own way, because they could buy every workingman of executive ability out of his class and make him a salaried manager for their own benefit and his, while they capered about the continent and planet. But at this period a sentiment akin to patriotism made its appearance in the breast of labor. They began to love their cause and to be loyal to their fellow-laborers; there were some who declined to manage for the traveling capitalists. The owners were stupefied by this innovation. Was it possible that anyone existed who would not sell himself for money, especially low-born workingmen? Was it conceivable that they must now manage their shops themselves, they who knew nothing whatever about shops or work, who were born for junketing and joy?

Some of the best managers replied to these lamentations and entreaties that they would assume the conduct of affairs if the workmen were taken into partnership, while if not, they would organize partnership shops independently.

"We always thought brains were with us," wailed a capitalist, weeping tears of blood—"not our brains, god forbid! but working-class brains, which saved us the necessity of having any, which we could buy,—and we have made the world ring with our prognosticating hosannas that brains would eternally come to the top, to us. We thought ourselves safe from co-operative aggression because the people's managers rushed to us like insects to a lamp. Oh, woe! Fidelity is dead! Brains desert the hand that has let itself be fed by them!"

"Hold!" said a manager; "the hand that let us feed it and ourselves that it might use us to take the food out of the mouths of our comrades. If we chose to continue the gormands your system has made us, we might receive the same salaries as now, and among the workers might be distributed your enviable portion. We should be as well off, the workers far better, and you who earn and deserve nothing, would receive your share—nothing. But we managers do not intend to remain gormands."

So the partnership enterprises grew, taking in the people who were thrown out by the failure of capitalist competitors, letting those who had not money to buy stock earn it by their labor, over and above the good support which they earned.

These successful partnerships had their inevitable effect on the old-style capitalist employers. They saw the field of production which they had owned entirely, and cropped for themselves during an indefinite past, slipping from their control. It was not, however, the capitalist who had always been saying, "we should like to make things better if we could, but we see no way," who followed first in the line the working people were going.

In consequence of their increasing property, the workers now began to have a voice in judicial decisions and legislation. A judge was offered a special train by a great railway corporation to go and sit judicially on one of their cases, but he refused it.

CHAPTER III.

THE GOOD DEEDS OF SOME CURTAILED.

Of course, long before this, discovery of what was called embezzlement in divers business houses had taken place, and the defaulting clerks had been sentenced to various terms of hard labor in the penitentiaries. They did not find the labor any harder than they had been accustomed to, however, and all of them began to improve in health and spirits from the physical exercise they were now enabled to enjoy. Their minds were free from care and they felt that they were having a vacation of life after the long hours and years of dungeon counting-house death. Some of them knew the little story of Maupassant's, of the old clerk who one day went out into the sunlight and discovered life, and hanged himself from the mortal sorrow he felt that the years had gone, and all the joy of the world had gone, and never had or could come to him. But these disgraced clerks felt no inclination to hang themselves. They knew that they had been great world-forces, and they watched with glad, half- realized hope, the mighty work which their sacrifices were sustaining, and their comrades found ways to keep them informed of the progress going on outside.

They did not need to concern themselves for their families, for the League attended to the support of such as had been able to save nothing from the meagre earnings of their bread-winner. But none of the employers' funds were used for this purpose. The comrades met such expenses from their own purses. The wives of the criminals were assuaged of their grief and chagrin by admission into the confidence of the League, and they felt proud of the courageous men who had done these things, and happy in the social degradation they endured.

The employers who brought these clerical appropriations to light, and their learned legal crutches, were painfully puzzled to trace the squanderings of the departed funds. Families of monastic frugality in walk and conversation with their neighbors must have been indeed clever rogues in spending never to show a trace of it. It was surmised that the peculators had also been speculators, and some solved the mystery by polygamic visions of various subsidiary families who now would come to want. The capitalists who lost most, denounced the robbers as atheists, and to make good the losses suffered, they increased their customary stipends to the judges.

The repeated recurrence of this total disappearance of the stolen moneys finally started one hyper-shrewd fellow thinking, and made him divine the existence of a secret embezzling philanthropic association of clerks. He called a conclave of suffering capitalists and imparted his discovery, expecting to be richly rewarded. He was astonished and mortified beyond recovery when they assailed him with derision. They said it was contrary to human nature as well as preposterously impossible to think that any man who could steal for himself would steal for the benefit of anybody else. They could speak from experience, which, like religious experience, could never be refuted. The capitalists had never been strained so to comprehend anything, and under the tension the meeting came near ending in a riot. The shrewd man went away feeling like Judas, but without the silver.

CHAPTER IV.

ORGANIZING.

In spite of these occasional digressions, the society went on its way augmenting. The membership reached thirty thousand. Many were clerks, many were people with moderate private incomes who devoted their entire time to the diversified works of the society. Every member pledged himself to the strictest economy in living, and to give all he could save to the social object. Spartan simplicity and primitive christian devotion characterized all.

The form of organization underwent sundry adaptations to the exigencies of growth and the ever more complicated labors assumed. Each city had its chief organizer, selected in every instance by the executive committee of the league, its four founders, and these chiefs chose organizers for each particular group. Secrecy pervaded like the ether. Only the high chief knew the members in his city; the group chiefs knew only those of their group; the members of a group knew only one another. The city chief passed finally upon every candidate proposed for admission. He also kept a chart of the group enterprises to save them from crossing in action.

To each high chief the under chiefs reported the application of their funds, and the economic and moral proceeds of their disbursement as far as they came into the exchequer of observation. These reports found their way to the central executive committee of the inaugurating four, who arranged, condensed and articulated them, in so doing preparing the intestinal social history of the period.

The original four still followed the arduous duties of their clerkship, not deeming it expedient to resign, because they were among the most brilliant abstractors. But the weighty work of conducting the great league was heavy upon them, for some of the larger projects, requiring general assistance, had to be centrally conducted by them. Therefore several secretaries, chosen with reference to their stanch honor, were trained for the service, and the private earnings of their associates preserved them from want.

CHAPTER V.

A FREE NEWSPAPER.

When this degree of perfection was reached, it was determined to take up the work of popular instruction. It was begun with the newspaper. The poorer people of the country, needing instruction nearly as much as the rich, were unable to subscribe for enlightening literature, and had nothing to read. There were also people of the other classes, in handsome numbers, who never read anything, and therefore did not know anything progressive, taking only the literary emanations from capital. The reform journal was therefore made like the starlight, free. Any one could send his own name and the names of all his friends and enemies, if he wished to enlighten them, and all from that day received the publication without price. The public was invited to meet the expenses of the sheet by contributions, and what failed after that was supplied by the league of embezzlers.

The plan proved an unspeakable achievement, and the subscribers' list mounted to a million the first month. Applications flooded in from every European country, and editions were prepared in each leading language. The edition, first monthly, was made weekly, then came a daily, afterward a review, as well as frequent books issued gratis. Having great wealth behind it and no fear within it, the journal soon possessed the ear of the whole civilized world, being terrifically reliable and reliably terrific at the same time. The other newspapers, appropriately called by one in those times the 'daily sewers,' saw their subscription lists shivered, and could not mend their fortunes even after curtailing their emission of garbage.

The mighty reform press was a veritable treasury of the keenest thought and fact, for now that there was money on the side of progress, the best thinkers changed their opinions very rapidly. Books and chapters and pamphlets of germinant energy were sown from this press among the people like wheat.

In less than a year the masses began to comprehend the meaning of those whom they had previously seen reviled as agitators and demagogues, and when they understood them they recognized that these monsters were the only wise people, and were right in saying that a change in the social order amounting to an absolute revolution was the only way to life. Many of the rich caught glimpses of the corners of this fact during dyspeptic retributions, but took more wine and said, "after us the deluge."

It soured the capitalists when they found themselves obliged to have the keen reform newspaper on their tables or never to know any news, for the superceded prevaricators of former days had been obliged by poverty to whittle down their staff of news-gatherers, and most of them had grown so sleepy that their buildings were used for cheap lodging houses. Thus the children of the capitalists were moulded little by little on the reform pattern, and the capitalists, seeing their own flesh and blood turning against them, felt as if they belonged to an extinct age and race.

Psychologists and historians of the new school frequently came to intereiew them to study their surviving mental processes for learned antiquarian treatises.

The great lying, gossiping, scandaling, advertising, sycophant, commercial, capital-serving sheets, went about now only as ghosts, through which their bones could be seen. Their absorber printed no advertisements for pay, its mission being to advertise the truth. Deceitful puffs of quack objects, vegetable, human and mineral, collapsed like a punctured balloon, having no bellows to inflate them. But in the League Journal appeared lists of all the new co-operative establishments, whether factories or stores, and the working people were advised to buy of these only, since their patronage would solidify such industries and compel others to follow their example. Agents of the capitalist producers offered fabulous bribes to be admitted to these lists, but as the editors were neither a legislative body nor traffickers in political, religious, moral, social, or literary opinions, the metallic persuasion had no gravitation in their scales. In the second year every city came to have a branch journal of its own, whose weekly issue penetrated each glade and glen of agriculture, tapping the trade of capitalists on that side.

CHAPTER VI.

LAWYERS NO MORE.

A literary innovation in this journal which speedily assumed consequence was the Department of Injustice. All cases where the weak had been wronged by the powerful, working people by their employers, the poor by the rich, were impartially examined, and if the charge proved true, the facts and the names of the oppressors were published. This let the offender down farther in public estimation and caused him more financial panic than a successful lawsuit at his heels would have done, and the poor and weak who never had seen an ounce of justice before, nor even known the color of the stuff, nor had the ghostliest chance of protection in the courts, now found redress easy, swift, telescope-aimed and costless.

This new engine of virtue spread contagious terror through the virtue-proof souls of those who had always made laws and enjoyed enameled immunity from them. Several such concocted mad slander suits against the journal, but the land-slide of evidence which the publishers had, compelled the capitalists and judges to flee from the case to come for their very lives. The infliction of wrong grew to be a precarious thing for the inflicter, and evil encroachments slunk away from the regions where this magical defender came. Publication was so prostrating to the delinquent that a mere private editorial notice to correct the wrong led to restitution.

Here is a case selected at random from the files: Three men whose families relied upon the wages of each day for bread, were hired by two wealthy land-owners to dig a well. The owners agreed to have bricks there for the walls at the proper time. The men cautioned them that the earth might cave if this were neglected. 'Go on digging,' said the owners, 'the bricks shall be there.' They dug as instructed, the bricks came not as promised, the sides fell in as predicted. It was Saturday night, they had dug two days, they asked for two days' pay. Said the canny owners, 'The well is not dug, and we cannot pay for its digging twice. When you clear out the hole again we will pay you the promised sum.' The men fasted that Sunday. They were workers of the lowest class and had no social 'pull.' The owners pulled the Sunday-school, the church and the community, with piety and money. But they received a note from the editorial Department of Injustice a few days after, and as nothing had yet been discovered which would pull that, the debt was settled the same day.

People of all classes soon saw what an unerring path to justice this department opened, and gradually they deserted the tedious, trickish, costly, squirming, capitalized courts of law. If the defrauders did not recompense their victims, the notified public dreaded to deal with them, and they found themselves in commercial coventry. To avoid the expensive loss of business and personal confidence, the dishonorable were often animated to reparation by a laconic notice from the Department of Injustice that their case was to be inspected. Thus while the volume of justice increased, the labor required to earn it decreased. No case ever arose where the impartiality of the department was questioned, since they had neither fees nor salaries nor railroad passes, nor any personal stake in the decisions.

Reason and equity decided the disputes and technical figments, which in the hands of bar and bench 'experts' always proved broad passages for Injustice standing erect to come in at and take possession, were barred up to be kept for specimen judgment-day testimony. It never took much time to settle claims on rational grounds, and the department was therefore never belated in its business. It protected itself and its clients from those who would knowingly prefer unjust charges, for those who were found guilty of this wrong, from malice or hope of gain, were themselves published in place of their intended prey. So only those who believed in their causes brought them, and those who had mistaken their claims were enlightened by the editors, and their minds being restored to equilibrium, and a cankering lawsuit of former days being averted, they adjusted their quarrel intelligently, and continued to enjoy life. On this side of its work the Editorial Board of Justice finally became a chamber of arbitration.

Naturally all this was a terrific catastrophe to the legal profession. Lawyers starved until they were obliged to work at something useful, and as some of them would not do this, they starved to death. Judges had nothing to do, and little by little nine-tenths of them were discharged. It was noticed that many of them became motor men on the street cars where their ermine was useful, or railroad ticket sellers where their majesty lost none of its frown or shine.

People now spoke their minds and said what they had previously thought, that the law was the most disreputable profession on the list after that of the hangman, and now they placed it ahead of the hangman's in vileness, because no one brought any cases to the lawyers which had the dimmest right in them, but only those which could be shored up by right-defying technical rascalities, calumniations, and the consecrated process of methodical lawful frauds.

The fetchers of these cases were low persons, devoid of the cranial elements of honor, and the attorneys susceptible to the blandishments of such simian scoundrels were obviously of the same family. The lawyer class was, therefore, as much despised by all as the prostitute class was by the women, and with more reason. The judges, of course, fared no better in public esteem, for every one saw that the lying technalists at the bar would have no chance if the judges did not abet them in their conspiracies to assassinate right by listening to their iniquitous verbal metaphysics. Moreover, if the brainless judges thought it their conscienceless duty to dip out what they labeled justice from the refuse of blinding, complicated statutes and precedents long dead and putrified, why did they not move to simplify these statutes, filter and boil the laws, and make the metaphysical legalities coincide with the true and the just?

The lawyers had always had unlimited chance to reform law, being not only its familiars and spiritual mediums, its vestals and pontiffs, and, therefore, the chosen ones to simplify and justify it; but they had been its manufacturers, very law-gods, out of congressional paradise sending their singing bolts. And what had they done with their super-terrestrial opportunities but build and dig a labyrinth in which to mesh and mulct everybody? No one had the least question why they had not been simplifying and disinfecting the laws for centuries instead of making the world bear their abominable carcass of diseases up the stony slope of time. Like every priesthood, the legal priesthood wanted a theology it could operate to the eternal salvation of itself from usefulness and the eternal damnation of others to the toils of supporting its uselessness.

Some of the law-moulding hypocrites who were left, now bethought them of sweeping away the ridiculous intricacies through which the people had always been gamed, plotting thereby to bring back an occupation for themselves which they could soon corrupt. They found no difficulty in legal lucidification—allegorical way-faring men could have done that; but when it was accomplished the courts of law had no more cases of any kind, for the rascals could gain nothing from a code of laws sound and sane, and therefore offered no more sacrifices to them, while the rest had no notion of putting themselves again into the jaws of the many-stomached judicial devilfish.

Desperate at the alienation of even the miscreants, the legal fog-makers made a final effort to reanimate the defunct haze and fraud; but the revolutionary journal followed each machination with such scorching exposure that the judges, several of whom were supreme bench fellows, — they, the unfittest, having survived longest,— became the laughing stock of children and everybody, surrendered to the inevitable, and retired to farms to recuperate their seedy stock. Then the courts were entirely empty and the profession of law became extinct.

A fabulous saving, both governmental and private, had all this time been going on. What had previously supported the creaking machinery of law was saved, and what had been squandered upon lawyers by litigants, was rescued to them. The legal maggot which had been a fearful ravager of every limb of industry, life and emotion, having its mouth everywhere, and being supported by the producers, was now dead. It was as if the expense of the great standing armies of the world were suddenly removed from the groaning people at home, and all the officery and soldiers of them began to produce. All the lawyers, clerks and court indignitaries had actually to do true labor. Production took an incredible bound, while taxes fell out of sight.

CHAPTER VII.

EDUCATION, FOR THE FIRST TIME.

Nobody will suppose that all this happened in a week. Other things had been going on in the meantime. This great free revolutionary journal had unceasingly advocated a rational system of education for the young. After the rays of the morning sun tipped the east of their minds, deputations of people from the masses, the middle class, and single individuals (disguised) of the rich, were continually coming to the editors imploring them to give their theories form and flesh and establish actual education, if only a little. At length they acceded. They did not hold immortal and sterile discussions ruminating the advisability, non-advisability, partial advisability, and impartial advisability of atomic alterations in curricula, goading their prodigious brains to invent surer means of enticing or compelling or narcotizing the youth to learn valueless things in a suicidal way, with a view to the wonderful eventual perfecting of educational enginery so as in due passage of centuries to have the steam up for the development of men and women. These revolutionary educators jumped the gutter of centuries, being of the mind that it was as weighty to save the children of the present as to let the race dwindle for the benefit of a dwindled posterity in some ultimate era. When people saw this so easily done — for it was only a matter of making up two or three minds to do it — they were amazed and wroth that the paid and provided educators had not done it in their grandparents' time.

They made a clean sweep of whole continents of educational rubbish, like Latin and Greek, and when called upon by the kings and heirs apparent of these extensive cemeteries, the professors, to defend their extraordinary want of consideration for the defunct, they replied by telling the very original 'savants' what they had never thought of before, that the Greeks became the wonderful people they were without the assistance of any language which was dead and buried Greek to them and their time, to rub and to 'sharpen' their faculties over, and saturate them with conceptions of a long out-grown period; while had they applied their brains to such deadly routine, they certainly would not have surpassed all other races of the world in the splendor of their originations on every subject they touched.

Their first care of all, beginning long before the cradle, was the health of the child, and this continued to be absolutely and unflinchingly first so long as education had anything to do with it. The second unalterable law was that the children should always be happy and never know that they were being educated. Anything and everything else might be sacrificed, but these things under no circumstances. The days of childhood are the time, they said, when one is most attuned to the pleasures of life and keenest to its pains. Childhood is, therefore, the most valuable and vital part of life, and other parts should be a preparation for it quite as much as it for others. To look upon this period as a getting ready time for grown-up years is, then, the crudest malpractice; it is like hearing the finer music first to prepare oneself to enjoy the poorer music more. Youth is undoubtedly the grandest time of life, when the powers are complete and full, and yet youth is mostly sacrificed in plotting and striving to get in more joy later on when the aptitude and faculty for joy have, like the clock, run down.

And, without any comparison of periods, each period has its own perfect rights if the full sum total of life is to be reached. To-day is as important as to-morrow; it must not be scrimped or scamped or sacrificed for to-morrow. It may be the day of a five-year old child, or that of a twenty-five or fifty-year old man; each is a day, with all present and past eternity, all possibility and reality crested in it. Life, when it is a perfect art, will focus and culminate all living in each day, as if it had been that toward which the process and motive of creation moved.

The inauguration of childhood and youth is the fair ideal, since, when each day is perfect, there can be no regrets and no additions, save the increment of a new and perfecter day to-morrow, born of to-day's completeness.

Meditating in this manner, these true philosophers asked if a lesson which spoiled to-day for the apparent sake of to-morrow, could make good its title to the desolation of to-day. Sir, to-day is gone, one gem out of life's coronet. Bring it back to me, the coronet is ugly without it. Can you not do it? Then you have impiously wronged me! Take one tooth from the fabulous perfect row that smiles to you; there are two eyes, beautiful in the vibrating lightning of their storied abysses. One will do; put the other out that it may be more beautiful. A ton of learning gained at the loss of one ounce of health is a dear purchase, did some one say? A ton of learning purchased by an ounce of sorrow is dear. Sorrow is a canker. Don't imagine that when it is gone it is gone. It scars and prostrates and haunts; it is a mutinous substance, unforgiving perpetually. For the benefit of a tree's beautiful to-morrow scrape the bark off on one side to-day.

No, children did not come into the world to learn lessons. The object of childhood is not preparation. The object of childhood is itself. How immortal the wisdom which beats the stars out of a child's firmanent that he may be fitted to enjoy the dead stars when he is a man! Now for life! When you are a man you may be persecuted by thoughts of death and separation. This generation's ancestry has been bad; we harbor evil forebodings and itch with the measles of immortality. Keep that venom out of children's ears. Death will overtake him all too soon, and he can investigate his own immortality. Teach him the wholeness and holiness of now, and discharge destiny of its religious mission to worry him. Let there be a great silence about Jesus and god, until he discovers that he himself is here in the universe with no secondary destiny. He will chat with the universe then on a fair footing. God is a great disturber of the peace, intruding himself like a child out of humor unless he is noticed. Did god place us here for the pleasure of nagging us?

Similarly there was no noise about the achievement expected of the child, no examinations, grading nor educational ceremonial of any description. The body of officious people formerly called teachers, who had soberly followed imparting and interference as a separate profession, passed away entirely, for all contributed, each in a natural way, not only to the development of the young, but of those less advanced than themselves. It was observed that the teachers, those high-tensioned hands of the educational factory, having altogether the most difficult, unappreciated and monstrously unnatural part to play in the intellectual industrialism of the time, were very glad to disappear.

CHAPTER VIII.

THE INVASION OF KNOWLEDGE.

A group of young men and women, seeing how things were going in society, organized a system of their own to go about teaching the common-schooled and untaught people. There were hardly any college students among these, and such as were of the college or university blue breed were those whom the professors loved least and pigeon-holed as educational vagrants. They were individuals with personality and a will not servile to their monitors, whom they declined to reflect. No professor was ever known to identify himself with this movement, or to say a good word for it, until the people were won over, when the professor class came into its arms stampeding. Nor was their accession then of any consequence, for one of the first things society did after the change was to dispatch that class.

No one thought of censuring the professors for their tardiness, any more than he thought of blaming miners for living in the dark. The professors' ordained duty was to drill the raw recruits for station in life and to teach all whom god intended to enrich with riches how to wring them dry into their private tubs. When the professors met any student who was not on a blind gallop after reputation, they were afraid of him, for they saw that if all youths were like that the moon of professoring would set. They said one to another that such an one's mind was out of joint, and devoted all their sophistry to sprouting 'ambitions' in him, whereupon, if these failed to root, they declared he was not educable.

The uneducable, therefore, united to spread the light they found burning in themselves and extinguished in the university dark-lanterns, over the groping American continent. They went singly from town to town with no money in their purses and no purses to make them think of money. When they came to a town they sought the most enlightened spirits, and found them always among the poor. To these they said, 'Show us how we may work and earn our daily bread—give us not our daily bread, but let us earn it—and call together the souls of your community who are loyal to light, and let us confer with one anther.' And in the evening, when the salt of that town was assembled, the wandering apostle of life said to them:

'The twilight of a new, miraculous day thrills the East. The sun lingers in his luminous chamber awaiting the order of ten thousand united wills to come forth. These wills shall say, "The sun shall rise *now;* by my soul it shall not wait for the generation of to-morrow, it shall rise by our compulsion. We will not live our lives in the night." The sun longs to rise. But it must have friends among mortals, and cowards are not friends. Cowards wait for others to act, the brave and true act themselves, to-day. What can the brave do? They can say, life should be lived thus and thus, and they can live it so. The apostles of the Nazarene workingman said, by putting ourselves under the four corners of earth and lifting, the earth will rise. They lifted and the mighty foundations of the earth split. In each village they gathered a few, and these in their tidal confidence were an army. Do likewise. Set your ideals as high as the stars; laugh compromise out of your hearts into the sepulchred domiciles of capital. Do all that thou canst for this mighty cause of life, give all that thou hast for it. Can the world be moved without power? Be yourselves that power. Be architects of a new society. You cannot delegate this task, you cannot pay men to change society for you.'

These and other words spoke the preacher scientists of a new order. And the people were stirred and met often to plan. They abandoned their old ideals of prosperity and lived in a simple manner. They had a common treasury into which each gave all that he could save from the needs of life, and these funds were used to spread the new conception of living.

Among the earliest of their acts was the building of a plain hall, to which all contributed the labor of their hands. This was always open and all speakers could use it freely for whatever subject they chose. It became a forum of intense intellectual and moral life. Since there were no limitations to speech, and every subject known to man could be sifted to its molecules, the intellects of the many who had hitherto lain dormant in churches and schools and shops began to wake up. They caught a glimmer of the wonderful world it was they lived in, and said to themselves, 'What helpless, hapless fools we have indeed been to pass through this fragrant, unspeakable garden of life as a traveler in a railroad train with the blinds down. The end of the journey is not our destination, the garden is our destination.'

So they set about transforming all the dead accumulations of science and experience into breathing life material. It was a hard task at first, and for a time it was feared that a civil war would be necessary to induce the scientists to impart what they had mountained up, for so insignificant a purpose as the improvment of human life. The object of science is to furnish the materials for books, they objected, and books enable teachers to have the appearance of wisdom and doctors to doctor. Science is not intended to modify the life of the crowd, but to give preoccupation to scientific brains which have passed through the transubstantiating mediations of learning. You say the institutions should be freely open to everyone to come and go as he pleases, without preparation, gradation, limitation or sequestration,—that would stand education on its head, place the shined professors under the inquisition of the swift, direct inquisitiveness of the vulgar, and democratize the aristocracy of knowledge in a shabby and indecorous manner.

When the people signified their intention to read in the libraries, and perform experiments in the laboratories, and watch the clinics, without certificates or antecedents or recommendations from anybody, the professors would have organized the students into military companies to protect their rights to these things unshared; but the students went home, not wishing to associate with illiterate persons, even as enemies in war.

Then a great raid was made on the locked-up literature, as western pioneers rush upon a gold field, each man seeking the shining lumps. They were astonished to find how much was insolvent dirt and rock, and could not understand why men of monstrous and renowned intelligence spent their whole lives picking the particles of these substances, apparently thinking that they were the gold; until they learned that it was a profession, following which night and day from adolescence on, the brains of these extraordinary diggers became lead poisoned, and everything at length looked precisely the same to them.

But the new prospectors refused to debauch their brains with dirt, and took the gold only. They selected what pertained to life in any manner, and especially the ingredients of physical and mental power and durability, and whatever would add to the happiness of any mortal while palaced on this planet, and these they imparted to the people assembled in the halls, showing them how to absorb into their lives the magic essences, to make them chyle and nutriment, driving out the depraved aborigines and making a mighty and immortal flesh. The children deserted the schools to come and hear, and as at all times there was some one discoursing simply, and other grown persons standing about eager to explain to the children in little groups what they did not understand, leaving them free to come and go as they pleased and enticing them with every form of instructive activity, they did not return to the schools afterwards.

Life began immediately with these children. A little useful niche was found for each, where he or she performed some pleasant industrial service, and feeling the responsibility of usefulness, his faculties grew alert and enquiring. Everyone was led whithersoever he desired to go, and beginning anywhere, around that beginning was gradually clustered a whole system of scientific knowledge and action. A child chose its own path, instinctively displaying its aptitudes, and to that path was brought everything which could further its progress and minister to its growth. The custom had formerly been to take the child up onto a mountain and point to a winding foot-way in the blue distance. Between were forests and murky swamps, rivers black and foaming, sand plains and rock-clad ridges, bottomless holes moss-veiled. Make your way to that foot-path, the educator said, and it will lead you somewhere.

Everybody now took a hand in educating, and their greatest delight was to go among the young in their games and lively studies, to learn from them and teach them, and to hear the noble cavaliers of freedom who had broken down the university ramparts for common occupancy, discourse. Love seemed to spring up among the people, and each sought to impart what he had to the rest, like a steadily burning star. Men and women forgot who were their own children, so interested and delighted were they in all, and the children ate and slept at the home where they happened to be, feeling toward all as toward parents, and receiving the tenderest care.

As there was no further use for the school buildings,

they were made annexes of the halls and used for educational purposes. In the summer time the halls and annexes were almost entirely deserted, for everything was done in the open air; and everyone became so strong and vital that a great deal of the working and thinking which had previously smelt of coal and carbonic gas was now performed under the airy ceiling of the sky and the thought-bearing smile of the juvenile, soft-skinned sun.

CHAPTER IX

TRANSFIGURATION OF THE CHURCHES.

When the crusading lecturers on life returned from their successful trip to the tombs of knowledge and began their Sunday impartations to the thirsty few who gathered about them, the churches were proceeding along the unrippled float of their dormitory eloquence. On their way home, much rested, some of the planks and beams of the ecclesiastical men-of-war occasionally dropped in to hear the closing words of a religion of life. They went home troubled in spirit and impaired in appetites, and returned the succeeding Sunday to hear the whole gospel. They saw how light of heart the new religionists were and what impregnable health had already taken possession of their bodies, and they said to their fellow planks and spars, 'This is the true church; knowledge adapted to life is religion; the enthusiasm to construct a grand, adorable earth is divine love;' and they joined the church of science, whose soul was human humanity.

As plank after plank parted from the armored fleet of theology, the cannons thundered terrific prognostications from the pulpits, pointing their muzzles straight at the simple wooden shells where Truth had taken up her abode. The next Sunday every lay timber in the ships went to view the corpse of Truth, after the sulphurous cannonade, expecting to see her perforated and jellied; but finding her alive and perfect, they tarried and were captivated by her words. There was left of the sacerdotal crafts nothing but the iron armor plating of creeds and the heavy-toned oracle guns, and while it is difficult to say which sank the other, both went down.

CHAPTER X.

THE WATERLOO OF "SOCIETY."

A curious change was meanwhile taking place in what is nomenclaturally known as 'society.' The rich had always found it simple to bow culture before the shrines of their dinners, and the excellent Mr. Emerson had said, 'To be rich is to have a ticket of admission to the master-works and chief men of each race.' Brains seemed to think that one of the reasons why it existed was to win its way into the society of the brainless. The man of money winked at the man of brains and the man of brains had an ecstacy. The women of money 'society' made lions and calves of the men of genius, and brought their friends together to examine the wonder, to feel of his ears and count his teeth, to adore and exclaim, 'Oh! our man of genius! our menagerie! our poodle dog! When the man of brains got as far as this, he thought he had lived to some purpose. His gigantic cerebrum, whirling with the joyous mesmerism of gleaming pottery and gems, to which — great god how wonderful! — he, only a man of mind and soul, was after toilsome years allowed revering access, could not hear the sardonic laugh of scornful condescension in the vacuums of these creatures of money where the soul of those soul-dowered is wont to sit.

The change originated when men of brains planted their first crop of character. It originated with the working people, where the soil was rich enough for character to grow. The leaders of this exodus from sycophancy and snobbery were those burglers of science, the outlaws who had broken into books and were distributing their booty every Sunday in the lecture halls. Seeing that they were 'extraordinary persons,' the rich society sharks prepared to swallow and digest them. They sent around to them those beautiful little missives of corruption and missiles of death — invitations to eat and be merry with them and marry. If they married the progeny of the rich imbeciles the eating imbeciles knew that the children of the combination would be bailed and neutered of genius, and property and imbecility would be safe.

There was crape on all the rich men's doors the next morning, for the extraordinary persons had refused to come to be digested, and the rich were mourning to think that they would have to intermarry their sons and their daughters one with another, and the descending crop would not stop on the perfectly decorous stage of imbecility, but would dip down to its legitimate levels of idiocy.

As feasts and bullion were substances which nearly all the great and noble characters of history had sought after as their befitting pay for being created great, the benighted possessors of these things thought that the extraordinary ones had perhaps not understood what they were being invited to, having recently sprung from the working classes, where nothing was known straight. So they held a meeting among themselves and appointed delegates composed of the most money to go to the extraordinaries and explain.

These bullion-ballasted tanks of expectation were ushered into the ante-rooms of the halls where the scientific highwaymen were beginning a wild joyous hour of play and instruction with the children, and were told to wait until the hour was over if they wished to confer with the extraordinary. They felt as they had always prided themselves on making delegations of workingmen feel when these came to plead with them for their underfed little ones. But they choked down their pride, for they realized with terror that if they could not prevail upon these vital men to come to their houses to be effeminated and routed, it was all up with their race and their uselessness.

When the hour was over and the religious bohemians learned who were awaiting them, they declined to confer with the petitioners, saying that the bright life of the day called them, and while breath was in them they could not think of dead thoughts or climb down into reactionary catacombs.

The rich men then decided upon a dazzling operation of generalship. They would endow the halls, for when the extraordinaries had salaries safe and perpetual dangling before their jaws, they would come down from the twig of principle like a shot bird. Therefore they put what acumen and property they could bring themselves to part with into an endowment, making it enormous in their desperation; but the lecturers refused to touch it, saying that the rich could keep their stolen possessions until tomorrow, when the people would take them all to endow the life of all. Many of the rich then made over the whole of their property to the common fund of the new movement, ceased bargaining for preference, and came as simple men to partake of the incalculable joys and beauties of true life.

When Homer and Buddha, the religion of Jesus and the aristocracy of Shakespeare, were long forgotten, the thrilling story of how a handful of brave men and women withstood the ever before conquering bludgeoning blandishments of 'society' on a high mountain and delivered the human race, was told to the marvelous magnificent children who sprang ages after from this deed of superhuman heroism.

When 'society' dreadfully gasped its last, a great miracle occurred, for the earth suddenly became four times larger than it was before, to accomodate the tremendous humanity which was about to be born.

CHAPTER XI.

POLITICAL PARTIES ALSO.

The most terrible affliction known to those days, after the dead evils heretofore recounted, was political parties. They were like a wild bull in a compartment with men without trees to get behind, and they were always doing something surprising and deadly. An enormous sum of treasure and sacred time was spent upon them, men voting and sweating and swearing and voting, and so chivalrous as not to let the women share the swear and vote with them. Every man whom they elected disappointed them, having hired his own election, so the rotatory multitude prepared to sweat and vote another personally nominated incumbent in. They kept this up like bats flying back and forth through the twilight, just for the sake of doing it, but mainly that they might sometime be able to buy themselves in; for those who turned the windlass of the voting multitude were few in number but mighty.

The first man who said it was not necessary to rule by political parties was imprisoned by his compatriots as a maniac, and many wanted to lynch him, for without the excitement of voting and getting angry and being disappointed and repenting, and doing it all over again as often as possible, they did not see how they could get their exceedingly vicious code of laws made more vicious. Nobody but a self-elected politician could come off more than conquerer in that emergency, and the sparkling-minded crowd therefore clung to him like a life-preserver. But the solitary man wrote books on the subject in his cell and dropped the leaflets about it out of the barred window.

Just at this time the first band of crusaders were returning from their pilgrimage to rescue knowledge from the university infidels, and they passed under the jail windows by accident. They saw the leaves flying there and carried them away to read.

'O perverse ones of this purblind generation,' read the book, 'do families manage themselves by political parties, or churches, or universities, or any great and prosperous societies? When you divide one of these into opposing factions to rule it that way, you may be sure its doom has been writ and undersigned by the shadows in heaven. But when it is a country all is different, and the littlest hamlets follow the national example, doing everything through a fight and spending more money to beat each other than the things would naturally cost which they beat each other to do. And yet after all why do parties exist? Is it not to get good and necessary things done in the best possible way? And if parties get the good things *not done*, and in the worst and evilest possible way, is it not clear that parties are a nuisance and incumbrance? That is what they do.

'As soon as a party organization is formed, the objects for which it was formed begin to be forgotten, and the mere avarice of success animates it more and more. Whatever originates from one party must be decried by the other, lest the people should think that the first party was doing a good thing and vote with it. Finally all the people are drawn into a barren conflict on one side or the other, and all receive a one-sided warp, being no longer capable of holding the entire situation in mental solution. They get the superstition that their particular party holds so much of the truth in its little sack that they must always keep their party in power, to prevent their dangerous opponents from having a chance to destroy the country with their depraved policy and heinous political machinations. While they are thus saving the country, all the good measures proposed by the other party are shelved, and as they themselves have no energy left after saving the country to propose good measures of their own, the country is being ruined at down grade speed by its magnanimous saviours. The other party becomes the saviour when it gets in, and has no time for profitable measures, and by and by they all reach a complete state of fossilage, hateful in the extreme to every honest and clear mind, and fatal in the extreme to the nation's weal.

'Then the good see that what parties started out to do they absolutely fail to do; starting to govern the country well, they not only govern it ill, they do not govern it at all, and they therefore decide to break up political parties. How do they do it? They first of all —'

At this point in the book the general of the jail discovered through informers what this seditious person was engaged in, and sent ten of his bravest assistants to put an end to it by placing the prisoner in chains. Thus it did not appear what they first of all did to break up political parties, nor what they did after that.

But the intellectual crusaders had learned enough. They said among themselves, 'The United States has now had the small-pox of political parties and seems in no fair way to recover. But if we can pull her through, she need never have that vile incrustation again. No man should belong to any party, except to a party pledged to act independently of every party and each member in it to act independently of every other member. There should be great proselyting for this Party of Political Freedom, which would end by being simply a Party of Freedom, and the only party, and then no party. For when they became numerous they would totally break up all party lines and machinery, for if no party could rally the people to it and hold a powerful contingent through thick and thin, good and bad, it would break up. Then instead of political parties there would be a country, a people. Their minds would be liberated from the overpowering mechanism of politics, and could search and weigh the reasons for each thing proposed; and thus being instructed and having no party hanging over them as a higher motive than the public good, twisting their judgment and will, they would unite to enact the good as any group of intelligent persons or a family does.'

There being no sentiment as yet in favor of such an all-embracing party of intelligence and freedom, however, the discoverers of the hemisphere of life determined to try the experiment among themselves, and to show in this winning and unanswerable manner what a round-about way society was traveling to reach nowhere, when a beautiful region lay near and straight before it. They therefore formed an embryonic state within the old state husk, the units of which were a new community in each community. These communities consisted of a number of friendly persons who agreed that politics was not a separate function of life, and that it therefore needed no separate attention. Having a separate politics was as if a farmer should call upon a neighbor to form his family and hired help into committees and bureaus to lay out and correspond and vote about his, the first farmer's, work. While the second farmer and his secretaries were doing this, the first one would be going on as usual with the work which was being legislated about, with the difference that now the farmer had to support not only his own farm group, but that which he had appointed to build air-castles and cast votes concerning it.

Abolishing all this pretty paraphernalia, they adopted the new code of life in which they believed, and began without preliminaries or authorization to carry it out. For instance, without waiting for the unsanitary officials to leave their duties unperformed through all coming time, they voluntarily took the procrastinated functions upon themselves as far as their numbers permitted. They invited any who believed in the usury of good health to join them, and this way of putting it won the throng who were looking for a good investment, and would have preferred typhus to helping them if they had called it the socialism of good health. In all things they were very sagacious about the use of words, and they found they could drag the public wherever they wanted to take it by the tag of a syllable.

For example, when they wanted to do anything with the co-operation of all, they advertised that they had a *laissez faire* plan on foot, and every business man sent a thousand dollars to aid the individualistic project. If they wanted to abolish a function of government they told the people it was paternal, with a squint of Socialism in it, and everybody went into a passion to abolish the function before night. By merely saying that it was anarchistic for the government not to own land and everything by which anything is produced, the people one day nationalized everything, men as well as shops and railroads and land, for they said men produced things and it was worse to have men who were anarchists than shops which were, so men must be socialized. The authors of this experiment next day remarked that it was not anarchistic but individualistic to have shops and land private, and immediately everything was unnationalized. Thus they played on the intellectual American middle and upper classes as on a piano out of tune.

The health of the community improved so rapidly under their sanitary management, that the public boards and departments, which had been drawing salaries and neglecting their duties ever since sanitation was discovered, resigned and left the field entirely to them. So they took one department after another out of the government or municipal control, first carrying it on in a small way among themselves, then having a great augmentation of numbers from those admiring the way it was conducted and wishing to enjoy the benefits of it. Government by that time being in a minority, was compelled by the ballot to turn the function over to them unreservedly.

Of course political parties had no part in this process except to fight it, but after they had been worsted in one thing after another and driven completety from the field in every important government enterprise, they gave up in disgust and their members turned respectable citizens.

They then built in every town and city a forum, or several of them, commensurate with the needs of the city, where the people could assemble and make one another's acquaintance, where they could loaf and enjoy themselves, each other, and the sun, where they could discuss, hear addresses, debate, and project and agree to public measures. The plain halls had grown to these, and for the winter use there were covered forums. Life became diversified and centralized; men's and women's eyes grew keen and beautiful; they were interested in life.

CHAPTER XII.

DISCOVERY ON A SUFFICIENT SCALE.

But in carrying the reader forward over results which occupied nearly a quarter of a century, I have left him in suspense about the fate of the organization of embezzlers to whose considerable exertions all these splendid transformations were due. Going back ten years events of a most portentous character transpired. It was then that the entire league was unearthed, fourteen years after its inception.

The discovery came through an accident of nature which the wisdom of man could neither provide against nor foresee. The private secretaries of the founders were as noble, pure-minded, zealous and reliable as the fathers of the league themselves. But their work grew so heavy that from time to time it was necessary to increase their number. So great was the caution required for a suitable selection, that a considerable period sometimes elapsed before the proper person was found. During one of these periods, when the burden upon the college of correspondents was uncommonly great, one of the secretaries was suddenly taken with an insanity which had slept in his family for two generations, and of which none of the guardians of the league were cognizant, the parents and grand parents of the capable and excellent man having appeared sound in every respect.

This secretary disappeared, and a week later certain

simultaneous arrests were made, two of whom were the League's founders. It was rumored about the country by telegraph that a stupendous organization of employes existed for the purpose of robbing employers. Everybody hastened to examine his books, and so many discovered themselves victims that a panic spread over the entire commercial population. Arrests were made to the number of hundreds a day. No man could tell but all his clerks were in league against him, and many an employer had his whole staff jailed. The officials and police lost their heads during that period, and no evidence but the suspicion of a capitalist was required to throw a thousand men into prison.

The frenzy reached its full fury when the police, being multiplied to ninety-seven times their usual number—which gave employment to workingmen—having been arresting night and day for a week, swept down upon the newspaper offices of the league and carried every editor off in irons. The total number of incarcerations hovered about 250,000 that day, although the society all told had but 50,000 members, and most of them had been omitted in the arrests, because of the confidence their employers reposed in their extraordinary fidelity. Some of the arrested ones who were not made of league integrity had been stealing a little on their own account, and thinking the whole disturbance was occasioned by that (for they had seen that the theft of a cent or a cotton handkerchief would throw a rich employer into convulsions of temper for hours), they believed that their doom had come. Those who, being extremely cowed by the industrial grandeur of their employer and his divine power to make beggars of them, feared that they might have stolen something without knowing it, were in a state of heart-rending grief and sent for their ministers, who, however, did not dare to come lest they should be thought to condone the criminals, and should lose the support of their employers. But there were several out of the quarter million who declared in wrath that were it not for the free food and the rest they were now having for a few days, they would fight the unjust scoundrels the employers and their system, when they got out, if they ever did alive.

The prisons did not begin to be large enough and the criminals were lodged in the school-houses, which were easily converted into keeps for the parents of those who were wont to be confined there. The children, on their part, hailed their liberation with ecstacy, cheering their benefactors — the police — as the school children of Budapest years before, freed by an epidemic of cholera, cried, long live the cholera.

The militia were called out, but most of them had been arrested and could not come. The regular army and navy were put in motion, for it was well known that their mummied minds were unflecked by anything relating to the progress of the times.

In the memory of the living only the days when Sumpter was fired against and Lincoln assassinated bore the palest resemblance to the lurid gloom of this period, and in the sinister annals of history there are few spots where such gnashing consternation is registered as settled down upon the American continent through that event. Business lay dead, for no man, not even a business man, thought of buying, selling or working in the silent but terrific excitement of the time.

The capitalist dailies came out in fifty-page extras each hour, spreading new particulars, most of them false. Every man knew intuitively that he was ruined and dared not face a microscopic examination of his affairs. No one doubted that hundreds of thousands of the plunderers were still at large, brushing against them on the streets and preparing to complete their annihilation of society. They expected the prisons to be stormed by these desperadoes, whereupon they were assured a universal massacre of themselves would ensue, and with money in their eyes they besought the authorities to execute the few captured culprits without delay or the formality of anything but a presidential proclamation couched in court-martial literature. They hoped that this suggestive step would avert the perpendicular drop to pre-adamite barbarism which would follow if the civilized and humane capitalists bit the dust, and they said the world might as well not be peopled at all as not be peopled by them.

The self-control of the authorities, including the president with his cabinet ills and chattels, was now beyond resuscitation, and these executionary measures of slaughter would undoubtedly have supervened had not one of the league inventors interfered. He sent word to the president of the Republic, requesting to be allowed to confer with his three colleagues in originality, for the purpose of allaying the crisis. The prayer was granted, under a strong guard of armed men and a stenographer. He proposed to inform the authorities of the existence of the league's annals, in order to put them in possession of the assuaging truth. He pointed out to his associates that the league had now accomplished its mission, and according to the solemn compact of each who had joined, all were now bound to face with steady mind the full consequences of their pioneering career. Death was staring at them darkly from gas-posts, but if they continued silent several times their number of innocent persons would perish also. He therefore advocated calling upon the chieftains of each city to notify all the members, through their group chiefs (where these had not been imprisoned), of their plan of preserving the Republic and saving the innocent from butchery, so that each might deliver himself up to injustice voluntarily if his soul moved him

This was done. Up to that moment none of the incarcerated leaguers, though pressed, prayed with, threatened, bribed and tortured, had revealed a fact. When the suggestion of the superior committee was authenticated to them, all went to the astonished officers of their employers' law and gave themselves up. The whole country was more paralyzed than before, for if fifty thousand of the most invincibly true, pure and beautiful characters alive had been chosen, these would have been the ones. Black flags and crape streamers were hoisted from the houses of all the capitalists to impress the populace with the sombre awfulness of this pulverizing collapse of human virtue, and they felt secretly that with such a fifty thousand-tongued example of clerical retribution it would never be possible for them to conduct their business of plundering with security again.

The ancient rusty press of the country, now that the great free popular press was silenced, had for the first time in years an opportunity to make a few coppers and be read, and was working day and night to give voluminous extracts, digests and photographs of the proceedings of the league, taken from the ten bulky historical volumes which the secretaries had compiled under the direction of the four patriarchs.

The law mercenaries and the capitalists now regained the courage necessary to release the two hundred and forty-nine thousand persons who had been wrongfully imprisoned, but when they saw the black looks which these persons brought out of the school houses in consequence of the sooty reputations they had received there, the capitalists stood in greater fear than before, and only saved their lives by having all these menacing individuals put on the extra police force where they could draw pay for doing nothing. This gave healthy employment for working people, whose support naturally had to come out of the private subscriptions of the capitalists. To appease their wrath and protect the capitalists, the clerk-police force was armed with the usual club and a revolver, and they went about drilling and showing great determination. The fifty thousand actual offenders in prison were entirely silent.

Of those released, a great many had been editors of the People's Free Journal, for most of these editors were entirely ignorant of the incubating process by which the grand news educators had been hatched.

These radiators of truth now began again their interrupted publications.

The epileptic dread of the rich having somewhat subsided again by the disposition of the reputation ruined clerks in a standing army of police two hundred and forty-nine thousand strong, and the tranquilizing discovery of limits to the dimensions of the defaulters' organization, the clamor for instantaneous death to the real criminals softened into a gurgling determination to imprison them for life and confiscate all the property of all as a slight reimbursement offering to the robbed, and to make their infamied children remember whose children they were.

CHAPTER XIII.

THE TRIAL.

The customary formalities of law were entirely neutralized in each mind by the actinic rays of vengeance which fulminated there, and the capitalists, who now threw off all the amenities with which they usually led the administrators of government and 'justice' about, ordered the president of the self-governing Republic to call his cabinet of executive tinkers and the distinguished shavers of the supreme bench together to settle the case as the capitalists required it without delay.

The capitalists said that an extreme sentence must be meted out to the astounding villains, and the boss commercialist of the white house and his journeymen said that it must. The capitalists said that the minds of all future generations of employes could only be rescued from fearful moral debauchery by the distribution of summary retribution, and the presiding executive mechanic said it was so. The capitalists nudged the supreme benchmen and whispered that the plebeian brains of their common servants the dress-deifying clerks must be terrified against the recurrence of such an unparalleled disaster, and the viscous intellects of the rest of the common people must be moulded into respect for law and the commandments of revealed religion, which the shocking magnitude and magnanimity of these atrocious crimes had shaken, by a woe-creating realization of the piercing sorrows the squadron of justice was prepared to saturate them with. The benchmen bowed assent in respectful silence, holding their hats and wigs and judicial scales in their adipose hands.

It was arranged for the trial to take place in the metropolis, but from centre to ends of the country none but indispensable activities were resumed and hardly anybody ate. The steady stillness and order of the common people was the subject of frequent encomiastic salutatory cannonading from the capitalist press.

The trial opened with the examination of the four founding patriarchs of the league, who were to represent the whole organization in trial but not in punishment.

"You may inform the Court of the grand aggregate of your defalcations," said the president of the Republic, acting as supreme pontiff of the compound tribunal, after having asked the capitalists if he might do so.

The founder to whom this remark was addressed, replied, speaking with a pivotal composure which made his excellency tingle under his skin: "Being employed by a Trust I succeeded in extricating yearly one million dollars."

President—Extricated! How long has this continued?

The Founder—Fourteen years.

President [with a deprecating gesture of consternation in the direction of the capitalists]—Do you mean to say you have robbed your employers of fourteen million dollars?

Founder—I have taken fourteen million dollars of the moneys that came into their hands.

[A murmur of astonishment runs through the court room and is echoed outside where the streets are blocked with people for miles away.]

The President [endeavoring to be satirical, but trembling]—Have others been as thrifty as you in unloading their employers' treasuries?

Founder—Those connected with Trusts have, in most instances, appropriated one million dollars a year.

President—How many of your excellent associates are 'connected with' Trusts?

Founder—Not less than three hundred.

President—Are we then to believe that not less than three hundred millions yearly for fourteen years have been stolen by your unprincipled imitators from Trusts alone?

Founder—I did not say that. Many of the Trusts have existed less than fourteen years, and the clerks of others did not join us at first. Our books signify the exact sum derived from each. The average annual transactions of the League have been one hundred million dollars; last year the income was nearly three times that amount.

The President [drily]—This is the story of a lunatic, or of one who would buoy up his cause by fabulous lying. You cannot impose on Us; industry would not have survived this prodigious exhaustion a month.

The Founder—[with the weary smile of one who

has shattered political economy against dull minds for many a year.] The books of these firms, when investigated by experts instructed in our method, will show. As to what trade or industry would bear, what we have done is better proof than theories about it. Society is in higher financial condition than it was before this tax for the benefit of the common people was levied. The more those you call the 'lowest ranks' receive, the better is the financial condition of the whole.

President [growing red and frowning heavily]—You are not here to give lessons to the Executive and the Bench in Political Economy. It is to be presumed that Ourselves and this learned body of Judges can speak on that subject with a little more wisdom than an ordinary commercial clerk.

[Applause from the spectators' benches occupied by the capitalists, and a sound of sibilant dissent from the aisles back of the railing, where the working men and women are packed, echoed again miles away. The president being too angry to collect his economical senses, the Chief Justice of the learned Bench takes up the questioning.]

Chief Justice—What is your salary?

Founder—One thousand a year.

C. Justice—How long have you received so much?

Founder—Twenty years.

C. Justice—And before that your salary was —?

Founder—Twelve hundred dollars.

C. Justice [turning exultingly to the capitalists]—You see he was a second-rate man whose deficiencies punished him with a reduction of wages.

Founder—All salaries and wages were cut when mine was:

C. Justice [moving in his chair]—How was that?

Founder—When the company consolidated with others in a trust, the salaries of all who owned no stock were reduced, as well as the wages of every working man and woman in the entire system of factories. The managers said there were plenty of people who would work for less than we received after the cut, and that their own profits must be in—.

C. Justice [dejectedly interrupting]—These details do not bear on the point. Your previous salary, you said, had been twelve hundred dollars for twenty years. A very good salary, I should say.

Founder—Allow me to correct you. I worked the first ten years for five hundred dollars a year. My pay was then raised to eight hundred. Five years after it was raised to twelve hundred. With the trust regime it was reduced to one thousand dollars, and no proposition has since been made to raise it.

C. Justice—That is a much larger sum than the great majority of artisans receive, and appears to me ample remuneration for mechanical clerical service. Capital deserves so much for the vast services she renders to industry by existing, that the working people will have to get along with less and less from this time on.

[Terrible groans are heard in the streets as these words are transmitted from mouth to mouth among the people. The Chief Justice continues:]

Will you now kindly tell us what part of the sums you extricated from the firm you so faithfully served you applied to the expansion of your private fortune?

Founder—No part.

C. Justice [putting on the well-known judicial severity like an impressive ulster]—You are speaking under oath, and though an oath could mean but little to one of your deformity, try for the sake of your country and the human race to speak the truth now.

Founder [laughing with fine enjoyment at the judicial bombast]—As every cent ever taken passed into the hands of our agents who gave receipts,—

C. Justice [interrupting]—Lying receipts!

Founder—And as these distributors have kept the strictest records of those to whom help was furnished, the honesty of these accounts could be pretty correctly tested. And what I say of myself is true of every member of the association.

C. Justice [with a sneering smile]—It is interesting to hear one with your record telling of his honesty.

Founder—But I will now say to you plainly, and for the benefit of all the working people listening to this trial throughout the world, that people who are meagrely paid for their services to the rich would be quite justified in 'stealing' from them on their own account and for themselves.

[Prolonged and thundering cheers follow this remark and shake the building. The capitalists are frozen with terror and the trial is delayed for some time.]

C. Justice [at length, turning to the president]—Your Sovereignty, I will relinquish to my colleagues the pleasure of conversing with this singular individual.

Another Judge [levels his pertified eyes at the criminal and proceeds]—Were you the originator of this plan for the wholesale seduction of property?

Founder—I was.

Judge—Inform the magistrates how, why, when, for what, and to what purpose.

CHAPTER XIV.

THE FOUNDER'S STORY.

The Founder—My father was a frugal, hard-working farmer, who finally underwent the fate so common to that class, and lost his land after a succession of mortgages. He had overworked for a long time to avert the calamity, and died soon after it came. I was then fifteen years old. A relative obtained a position for me in a city store. My mother could not see me go away alone at that age, breaking up the family, and as her own home was gone she accompanied me with the three younger children. She had expected some rich town friends of her earlier years to help make the way easier, but they forgot her. We lived, as we had to, in poor quarters; my mother sewed; our joint wages barely kept us. Within three years two of the younger children died. I had then learned book-keeping and secured my present position. We lived better upon my five hundred dollars a year. My remaining brother entered a factory, but never was strong enough to make the best wages, his constitution having been impaired by the privations of our first years in the city. Tenement house and factory life continued to bear unfavorably upon him, and at the age of twenty-seven he died, leaving a broken-down wife and two children, whom I sent to a country town and mainly supported until the children grew up. On account of these demands on my income I never married.

I naturally asked myself if it was necessary for people to be crushed and suffering—burdened through life as I and those near to me had been. My employers counted their wealth in millions; each owned several sumptuous houses and lived in the tropics of luxury. I knew of a great number of business and idle men with similar possessions and similar habits of life. Pondering these disturbing contrasts, I discovered a clue. If these millionaires, greater and less, would set aside annually in the ratio of their possessions a sum for the simple, designed, chosen, express purpose of altering the social foundation upon which the poor stand, and would themselves, with the same interest, energy and intelligence they display in commercial affairs of their own, originate and carry forward such an alteration, or would appoint intelligent and capable agents to do it, as they choose agents in their own business, there would soon be neither occasion nor possibility of such a life as mine or of such death as had pruned my family down.

I reasoned that the rich could spare enough for this beautiful end without curtailing a comfort, and, absorbed in my vision of the ineffable happiness and power of life and character they would bestow upon innumerable others by these slight sacrifices, I dreamed that it was only necessary to reveal to them the marvelous commission they held to lead the old world many a day's journey toward paradise and perfection, to start in them an earnest and perpetual fondness for this benign generalship.

I arranged a lucid plan, showing, 'with a little money this can be done, with a little more that, and with yet more these fifty excellent inventions can be mobilized, and by the time they are in action half of the poverty and suffering will capitulate, and in less than twenty-five years the whole face of the earth will wear a renovated and unrecognizable aspect.' I set forth in columnar demonstration—being a man of figures and business—the sums which could be spared from domestic expenditures by the capitalists to meet this outlay, and proved that there would be a surplus for theatres left.

Having thus fastened the plan together with unbreakable bands of fact and screws of reason, I approached the emotional side of the subject and wrote a sagacious paragraph on the cogency of commencing this grand sociological migration under the stimulating conductorship of the great capitalists, for if they initiated it, so commanding is the authority of true worth, high character, bottomless brains and cyclopean wealth, that the men of littler worth, character, brains and property, would speedily get into the procession. This paragraph I reserved for the richest, and it won me many warm admirers, offers of personal advancement, scholarships in the universities which they had to dispose of, and the management of newspapers, especially if I would write leading articles setting forth my opinions on this subject.

I managed to shut all these flattering openings with my next sentence, which implied in the most etherial language I knew, never an unambiguous word being used throughout the whole, that a revolution was walking the capitalist's way, which might reach and destroy him before he heard of its existence if some good-hearted person like me did not act as sentinel to warn him.

I then came down to strict oratory and told the capitalists with impassioned utterance that they were the ones and the only ones who could save us from the danger of violence. 'Think of it!' I cried in mighty wrath, 'The wealth of the country, the shops and railroads and everything else are under your control and owned by you. You are conducting these things in a manner which brings absolute ruin upon a great many, and wretchedness, disappointment and collapse of hope upon a great many more. Can I change this? I do not own the things. Can the middle class change it? They again, are only small, uninfluential owners. Can the working people, those who are suffering most, change it? No; for you and not they own and operate the causes of their sufferings. And you, *you could change it, can change it when you will;* you can avert the violent rising of the masses which is possible. By applying the wealth which the masses have made for you to placing industrialism on a different basis and carrying society wisely through the transition it is about to make in some manner to a higher plane, you could render some recompense for the prodigious wrongs you have done the poor in degrading them by robbing them, some recompense to society for bringing it to the edge of destruction.

'You are responsible, you rich, you capitalists: not you as a system, but you personally, each one of you. You are public enemies. You can only redeem yourselves from this stain by acting soon and undoing the infamous hurt you have done all. You, then, I brand and attack. You, each; not a shadowy impersonal thing called the 'social system.' You board and bed the social system, fire it up and run it, own, manage and milk money out of it, and then you plead innocence of its crimes! Oh, blameless ones, you are the murderers of everyone murdered by this system, the cause of all the terrible ruin to human beings it accomplishes. You are the dire, callous, devilish cause. Repent and turn your stolen riches to undo this, or the down-trampled, infuriated people will find you out, and then what?'

Armed with this subtle document I visited the capitalists, going first to those who employed me. The great leading man in our concern, who had worked himself up to that summit by the death of his father, was affable, listened to my sketch and then to what I could say in its favor, restraining his deliberating judgment until all was through. Then he spoke, and I saw how it was that he was such a power in the world. "You have excellent ideas," he said in measured, anathematical tones, and the north star seemed to revolve about him, "but they are not practical. In two or three thousand years they may be practical. As an irresponsible clerk everything looks extremely simple to you. My great responsibility on your shoulders for just one day would crush you to atoms, and you would understand why it is not practical. Responsibility opens one's eyes and makes him practical. Now I am practical; and just in a practical, friendly way I must advise you not to spend too much time flying your little theoretical kites and telling people how to improve. We don't want people to improve, we want them to work, and you belong to that number."

He had reached ground where he was at home, beating the brains out of working people according to the scriptures of industry; his concentrated eyes bulged, and lest they should split or fly out of his head at me like bullets, I thought it was time to go. Where was his affability? I had forgotten that I was only his workingman.

I was not discouraged. For several months, after hours, I wandered on my pilgrimage among the capitalists. Some refused to see me, saying their time was too precious for the contemplation of charitable objects; some were wroth because they averred I threatened them in saying that they and they alone held the key to the situation and could avert violence, and they declared I ought to be imprisoned to keep me from spreading my ridiculous nonsense about them; a third lot took it as a good joke. "My good fellow," said one, "these working people get all they deserve. They would spend the rest in drink and idleness."

I replied I had never heard any one say that before, and asked him if he thought that I, who had lived long among the poorest and had been one of them, ought to know.

"Ah, but you don't know as well as I do," he responded."

"But how do you know?" I insisted.

"A member of my family who represents intellect,

and is in fact a trained intelligence, keeps an eye on the slums," he said.

"Read this," I remarked, passing him an editorial from the London *Times* on the subject of a new free library in East London.

"It won't change my mind," he answered, but he read it.

"In the first place," he read, "people whose earnings are such as to make every six-pence spent a serious matter, cannot buy books, even cheap ones. In the second place—and the consideration is still more important—if a whole family has to live in two rooms, there is neither room for the reader nor for his books; nor is there likely to be much of the necessary quiet."

"The *Times* was never known to embellish the barrenness of the poor," I suggested. "There are 'whole families' that have to live in two rooms."

"I know how to answer that," said he. "I've heard it answered before."

"How?" said I.

Said he, "That is in London, not in America. This is a free country and we do not have such things. And if we have them it's the fault of the two-roomed people, who have not brains to earn more than two rooms. There's nothing bad about living in two rooms either. The intelligent member of my family has found plenty of families, children and all, living in two rooms and perfectly happy, contented and religious. Go to Europe with your plan, for it is not needed here."

"Do the two-roomed people read?" I interjected.

"Read?" cried he, "why should they read? I don't read?"

"Break your rule and look at this," I said.

"Is it long?" queried he.

"The words are not long," was my rejoinder, "but perhaps I had better read it to you."

"Do so," he acquiesced.

I read:

"The testimony of Mr. George R. Humphery, who has been in charge for twenty years of the books read by factory people in England, in regard to their reading habits and opportunities is worth something to the thousands of persons in New England who are connected with the factories as operatives, and who have limited opportunities for reading. He well states the difficulties under which any trustworthy and successful work is accomplished by the industrial classes. In the first place, very few of these people can afford a separate room for study. Again, they are constantly compelled to work overtime, and this interferes with a regular course of study. It either prevents the attending of classes at an evening school, or it renders a man unfit to read at home. If the men are serious to become masters of their trade, they must spend some time in the evening in working out problems that have perplexed them during the day. They are often without work, and the difficulty of obtaining new positions interferes with their regular acquisition of knowledge. All these drawbacks interfere with the regular reading or study of the working classes. They must be remembered when we consider what it is possible for them to accomplish.'"

"Would you like some more?" I asked.

"I didn't ask for any of it," said he.

"Take a little more, then, while you have the chance," I remarked; and I recited a few more extracts about "these people."

"'It is only a limited degree of reading that is possible to our factory population. . . . The most that can be done for the intellectual improvement of these people is to supply them with such works of fiction or biography or of popular scientific exposition as are within their comprehension. . . . For the most part the readers among the working classes are persons who are not prepared by education to take up what is profound and thorough.'"

"What agitator wrote that incendiary stuff?" he questioned contemptuously.

"The Boston *Herald*," was my answer; "April 13th, 1893."

Said he, "It's terrible when a reliable capital sheet prostitutes itself like that. If these silly newspapers do not keep the truth out of sight a little more skilfully we shall take a header into chaos."

"So I said in my epistle to the capitalists," I added.

"But not in your way, and not by our fault," wailed he. It'll be because the common people do not know anything and want to own everything."

"Give them a chance to read and learn," finished I, quitting him.

By this time I thought it trying enough to visit native capitalists without attempting European ones as I had been bidden.

The next one gave me a dissertation on my one-eyed way of looking at things. "Open the other side of your brain," quoth he, "and use that awhile. Go and improve the people; spend your energies that way; make them meek, teach them obedience to their employers; don't be finding fault with us rich, world without end. I'm tired of hearing it. Fault-finders never accomplish anything. Tell the common people their duties to us. They don't work half as much as we want them to; they are not faithful. The trouble with them is they need religion. I haven't any opinion of your plan, but let me tell you you must be broad-minded and all-sided or you can't get any influential person interested in it."

After this I reflected a few days, having learned something. I had been a child before. Now I was a man. I had ascribed the conduct of the rich men's lives to their ignorance, thinking that if they knew the hell they create and keep in running order and temporally eternalize for the working many of mankind, they would swiftly stop its mouth up, close its furnaces, and fill up its lakes. Now I knew better. I now saw that they were determined to live on as they liked though hell ate up the poor here and hereafter. Now I realized that their course of life was deliberate, intentional, planned, and the cause of it I realized — impregnable selfishness, irreducible indifference and a petrifaction of soul not to be dissolved or granulated.

The winged truth sped through my mind that if I went to the ocean and prayed and appealed to it, I should accomplish more than by appealing and paltering to the rich for justice, humanity and restoration to the poor. "Abandon our luxuries, abandon one luxury to give those coarse, remote, servile animals, the common people, food and decency and happiness and life? We the hyper-excellent, drawing-room distilled, soul-washed-and-ironed, blood-desiccated, picked-over and sieved for two generations like skimmed flour bereft of its wheatfulness,—we, the capitalists, abandon a privilege or luxury for the unsifted proletarian slum-soiled millions living down in the bowels of nowhere? No; the earth is ours and the fulness thereof, ours shall it remain forever and ever."

"Yes," repeated I, without knowing what I said, moved by some power in the elements about me. "Yours it shall remain while the clammy sky of the slums coagulates the brains of the anthropoid fishes who swim in those gases; but what if they should rise to the light and read the sacred message of resistance?"

I was very much disheartened. To confirm my despondency came a notice from the shrine of the tabernacle of the trust where I sacrificed myself, that my place would be needed for someone else if I continued to stir up the social sediment with the broken reed of demagoguery. 'You have not neglected your duties,' oracled the note, 'but you are busying yourself with things which not concern you and may make us poor indeed; you are making yourself a target of ridicule in the decorating eyes of the financial archangels.'

It had already ceased. 'Go with your staff of progress to stir up the capitalists to righteousness and public salvation,' said I, 'and it will be with you as it was with the man who went to stir up the philanthropic sentiments of the surface of the sun.'

But they had vowed that nothing could be done, not if they gave the money to the new laying of social bed-rocks, not if they gave ten thousand times ten thousand more than they had to give. I concluded to show them what could be done. You know the results.

CHAPTER XV.

SENTENCE.

The Judge—The results! Yes, you have corrupted society, you have undermined respect for law, you have struck a stunning blow at morality and religion; for you have robbed, defied the commandments, trampled on sacred Trusts, and all the good you falsely lay claim to springs from this million-fold greater evil!

Founder—What we have done was not robbery.

All the Judges [in great excitement]—What is that you say? Have you not taken millions which did not belong to you?

Founder—We made ourselves the agents of those who were robbed and overreached to restore to them their property. If a man steals your pocket-book, and I, without the knowledge of the thief, take it away from him and return it to you, am I a thief?

Judge—This is rank anarchist absurdity! No one has stolen but your precious crew. The rich whom you call robbers have broken no law or they would have been prosecuted and imprisoned.

Founder—What if a party of thieves formed the strongest element in a community and made a law saying it was right and legal for them to take the property of all men:—would that make it right?

Judge—No.

Founder—And if some other men secretly took from

the law-makers and robbers what they had legally wrenched from other citizens and returned it to them, that would be right ?

Judge—It would.

Founder—That is what we have done.

Judge—A fine argument so far, but I am waiting to see how you make out that the rich are the robbers.

Founder—Any man who takes and uses for himself more than is necessary for his life and health and development, or for the life, health and development of those dependent on him, while others lack what is necessary for their life, health and development, is a robber.

Judge—Ah, you say this, do you ! And these are your fine principles !

Founder—Yes, and I will not be so vague either, for the opportunities of all must be equal and he who would make *any* of them private property while others have less is a robber.

Judge—Such doctrines would destroy the foundations of property and wreck society. People of your depraved stamp are only fit for the mad house, the prison or the gallows, and I think the prison will be the place for you.

Founder—I have done my life work and now it matters little what comes to me. We have proved by a right application of a *portion* of the surplus wealth of society, that society can be radically transformed, the individual members of it made infinitely more virtuous and intelligent, and suffering and misery caused almost to disappear in a few years. What would the whole surplus luxury-wealth of the country do if expended thus? I now realize that a century of such expenditure would do for society what it is wholly impossible to imagine, for I apprehend it would produce of mankind a race as far above us as we are above the variegated African-Ethiopian in his primitive jungle. What you do with us will only brace our work; the fruits of it will be ever greater, never less.

CHAPTER XVI.

THE PEOPLE, AT LAST.

[It is the following day. The place is the same, and the streets are more densely packed, for millions have been arriving from every direction during the night.

The president of the Republic has recovered his sanity and composure and opens the court.]

President — We have conferred during the night and discussed the uncontradicted testimony obtained as it were from the very teeth of your conspiracy. We feel our station somewhat elevated in life — although that could scarcely be unless crowns were placed upon our heads — elevated by the sublime destiny centripetalized in us as vindicators of God and Abraham and Moses and all the owners of property since their time, as well as of the divinely inspired writers on the subject of property. We seem to be chosen instruments to pick the fragments of morality up out of the slime into which you have cast them, and to write again the ten commandments for the future on tables of immortal gold. How great should be our reward in heaven for this service! greater still our reward on earth [the capitalists applaud], and our names should be enscrolled with those of Lycurgus, Jeremiah, William the Conqueror and other legal sages. ["They shall be, we swear it," whispered the capitalists, "it won't cost much."]

To tie down virtue on this planet, which was about to fly away dismayed at your blaspheming, we consign your fifty thousand bodies to fifty thousand dungeons while they live and to fifty-thousand doctors when they are dead, and we decree that your entire worldly possessions shall be turned over to the capitalists who have suffered from your gigantic flintiness of heart.

One of the League — They 'll not get much, we used our property for the good of the race.

President — And we further ordain that all properties such as printing presses, buildings, co-operative factories and the like, which can be directly or indirectly traced to funds taken from employers shall be turned back to them.

A Man in the court room — This will ruin the people's journals !

Another Man — And keep us from knowing the truth about anything, as it used to be.

[As the judgment makes its way outside, groans are heard which finally become so terrible that the court windows break.

President — And finally be our will known, that whosoever has received aught of these capitalists' moneys, whether women, children or strikers, shall be holden to reimburse these sums, and the titles of all farms and houses which have been purchased for the poor in any place shall be made over to those from whom the money to buy them came.

A Woman — Now we are undone indeed. My house will go.

An Old Man — Oh this cruelty ! The capitalists will own everything.

Capitalist — Now that is justice. Our protectors cannot be intimidated.

Second Capitalist — It serves them right and is none too severe. I would have had the four ringleaders strung up. It's worse than murder to attack property. I shall be fifty million dollars richer after this.

A Voice [cries exultingly]—How will it be known whom the stolen money went to help?

[The jaws of all the capitalists drop; the president, cabinet and judges look as if they had lost a year's salary.]

A Bright Man in the crowd — The volumes of the League's records will show that, at least the Founder said so.

The Multitude — Destroy the records! Destroy the records!

[The capitalists gather round the records — which are in the court room — in a body, and the president commands the regular army to prepare to fire on the crowd. Word is sent to the police, including the two hundred and forty-nine thousand who had been unjustly jailed, to prepare for a general slaughter.]

A Capitalist — A lot of these people ought to be killed. If we don't make an example of them now they'll never give us peace and profits again.

A number of working women [jostling the capitalists] — You are the ones who ought to go to prison.

A Woman [shrieking at the top of her voice to the working men] — Oh you cowards!

Capitalists [in low tones among themselves] — This is pretty serious. It is time to shoot.

Another — Yes, blood always brings the scum to its senses.

A Workingman in the court room—Think what these men have done for us.

Second Workingman—I would rather go to prison for life myself.

Another—The capitalists will soon have us down on the ground again and then under ground. This is damnable! I can't stand it.

Another [stamping]—If American workingmen only had some of the blood of the Belgians in them!

A Foreign Workman [calmly looking on]—American workingmen are the most cowardly in the world.

Several Women [forcing their way through the crowd in a frenzy]—It's a lie. Before to-day's over you'll know whether they're cowards!

The President [mounting a chair]—I command the crowd in My name to disperse on pain of death. The officers will conduct the prisoners to their doom.

A Woman [in hysterics]—That man saved my children from starvation when my husband died.

One of the Regular Policemen—Some of those fellows looked after my sick father when he lost his job and the landlord turned him on to the street.

Ten thousand men on the outskirts of the crowd [from the West, armed with shot guns]—Did they say we were to give our farms to the capitalists?

Another squad [approaching in the distance]—Oh no, not yet!

The President [stepping on to the table]—Take them to jail, I say!

249,000 arrested clerk-police [sullenly]—If we go back to clerk for these capitalist robbers we'll steal everything they have.

The Crowd outside—We'll not desert our friends.

The Capitalists [to the policemen] — Do your duty and take these villains to jail.

A Policeman [throwing down his club] — I'll have nothing to do with it.

Other Policemen [following his example] — Nor I, nor I. We've served you rich swine long enough. We'll be bull dogs for you no more.

Capitalists — Swine! Do you dare call us swine? Remember we can hang you..

Policemen — Animals who take all they can get and leave others who cannot crowd their way to the food nothing, are swine.

Capitalists, president and judges [frantically] — We'll double your pay!

Policemen — It's too late. You can't hire us now. We're done working for money bags. We'll work hereafter for justice and the people.

Chief of the armed 249,000 — And you've got to settle with us yet!

[The noise without increases.

Later in the day the capitalists, president and judges, with a few militia-men composed of butlers and footmen, together with the regular army and navy, have fled to the banks and newspaper buildings and barricaded themselves in as best they could.

Immense throngs of people surge through the streets, cracking the walls of the buildings with their momentum. Meetings of the multitude are being held in the squares and over the country for fifty miles out.]

Speaker [to the people:]—

For twelve years we have been living in light and hope. We knew not what was doing this for us, but now we know. Shall we abandon those who made the noble venture and mighty sacrifice for us, who took freedom in their hands, scorned fate, and devoted their lives to making human beings of us?

A Thousand Voices — No! No! We're not such poltroons!

Speaker — Shall we allow ourselves to be forced back to that degradation and slavery from which we and our class have been lifted for the first time in this earth's annals?

The Crowd [in long resounding cries] — Never, while one of us lives.

Speaker — Then we must put an end to capitalism now. We must finish that old accursed system from which we have so long suffered. There's no half way work possible any longer. Our old masters will grind us to powder if we give them the upper hand again.

The Crowd — Down with the masters! Down with capitalism!

Speaker — Then let us send a deputation to them, giving them their choice. Either they may yield peaceably and unite with us to organize society on a just basis, or we notify them that we, the irresistible people, will proceed to that work without them.

Many Voices [amid earth-shaking cheers] — That we will! That we will!

[*Scene*—Before the Stock Exchange, which is the principal capitalist fort.]

Spokesman for the Capitalists [from an upper window. The president and the regular army stand behind him for protection] — What if we refuse your demands?

Working People— Then we shall ignore you and set about completing the transformation of industry which the men you have sentenced to prison have carried so far and taught us how to carry farther.

Capitalist Spokesman — Will you confiscate our property?

Working People —It is not yours. We shall take the property you abominably call yours, which you have accumulated from us and through our labor, and make an equal partnership, where you will have a voice if you choose, but no more influential voice than anyone else.

C. Spokesman — We will prevent that with arms. We will die sooner than give up what is ours and make terms to ruffianly social dregs and marauders.

Working People — To every hundred of you there are a million dregs. You can do nothing. No one but the automaton army will sell himself to shoot down the people of his own class and blood for your benefit again, and the people can destroy the army if necessary in ten minutes. You had better think twice.

Capitalists [quaking among themselves] — It is true, we had. We are lost.

C. Spokesman [to the multitudes] — You have no competent leaders without us.

Working People —We are all leaders now, since we have had a little education. We'll have more education. We'll never give our bodies and destinies again to bosses in this world!

C. Spokesman— But how can industry be organized on an equality? It is impossible. It would lead to chaos. No one would save. The idle would live on the industrious.

Working People—That is what your newspapers have always been saying, but the hundreds of mills which the working people have come to own on that very principle of equality since the League of Justice began to distribute wealth a little more fairly, prove that it is a lie. Working people save if they have anything to save for and anything to save from. The idle who have not inherited too bad an organization as a legacy of the capitalists' regime are put under special conditions of labor, and the really and thoroughly bad are soon singled out and treated like the sick which they are. Then they are known and treated and cannot impose on the rest of society, as they could under the old social misarrangement.

Capitalists [altogether; their eyes suddenly filling with beams of hope]—You'll at least leave us our land and railroads and such things?

Working People [with scorn]—We'll at least leave you nothing of the sort. This is not a play revolution. We propose to have the sources of wealth on this earth used for human good, hereafter, not for your private amusement—you, a little shiftless group of enormous spendthrffts, bragging ever and ever more of economy and abstinence.

Capitalists [after earnest and protracted consultation in which the army chaplain is several times called upon to offer prayer]—It is clear that we are beaten, and we might as well make the best of a situation for which there is no help.

[They come down into the streets and are greeted with cordial hand shakings and thundering cheers by the people.]

A Former Capitalist — I see how the factory that was mine can be run in common, give the largest possibility for the initiative of all and not for the manager only, and have the proceeds shared for the best development and happiness of all too. I knew how this could have been done all the time.

Surrounding People [hilariously] — Oh, we know how that can be done! But none of it to-day. Let every man, woman and child work for the banquet to-night! There never was a day like this!

Another Former Capitalist — This is life! I've been a dog all my days. I'm glad the change has come. I'm tired of slave-driving the working people. I breathe for the first time now, and so many good years gone!

People — There never was a day like this!

END.

CPSIA information can be obtained
at www.ICGtesting.com
Printed in the USA
BVHW040014040419
544577BV00003B/638/P

9 781313 278294